Tam and Sam

Look Around

By Jeannine Duch   Illustrated by David Sheldon

Target Skill Consonant Ss/s/
High-Frequency Words *have, is*

Scott Foresman
is an imprint of

Sam is at the tree.

 Tam is at the tree.

6 I have six bugs.

1 One bug is silly.

 I have a butterfly.

The butterfly is little.

Sam sings to six bugs.

Tam sings to the butterfly.